Original title:
Life's Purpose: Whatever You Want It To Be

Copyright © 2025 Creative Arts Management OÜ
All rights reserved.

Author: Fiona Harrington
ISBN HARDBACK: 978-1-80566-182-5
ISBN PAPERBACK: 978-1-80566-477-2

Horizons of Hope

In a world of dreams, we chase the sun,
With ice cream cones and laughter, just for fun.
Wearing mismatched socks, oh what a sight,
We dance through the day, our hearts feeling light.

With kites in the sky, we sail on the breeze,
Believing in magic, as easy as cheese.
Paint your own story, let colors collide,
In this crazy game, take it all in stride.

Mirrors of the Soul

Oh, mirrors reflect what we wish to see,
A dancing chicken or a wise bumblebee.
Check your hair, they say, but don't take a chance,
Lest your reflection breaks into a silly dance.

The table is turned, it's us who are fun,
Counting our giggles, till the day is done.
With hats made of fruit and a grin that's wide,
We waltz through the chaos, with joy as our guide.

The Light You Create

Shine like a disco ball, spinning around,
In a world full of frowns, let laughter abound.
Light up your corners, let sparkles take flight,
With crayons and giggles, we'll paint the night bright.

Embrace silly moments, they're fleeting like dew,
Juggling life's lemons, make lemonade too.
With friends by your side, bring joy to the fray,
In this carnival ride, make it your own way.

Footprints in the Sand

From giant footprints to tiny little hands,
We roam through the giggles, ignoring demands.
Skip like a stone, let your heart be the guide,
Leave trails of sunshine, let joy be your stride.

With jellybean dreams and a wink from the moon,
We laugh at tomorrow, dancing to our tune.
In the sand we write stories, so free and absurd,
Let every footprint say: 'You've really heard.'

Painting with Shadows

With a brush of laughter, I twirl and sway,
Creating worlds where socks can play.
A dance of colors in the air,
Let's paint the shadows without a care.

In the corner, a cat starts to prance,
While unkempt hair joins in the dance.
The table spills secrets, oh what a sight,
In the gallery of dreams, everything's bright.

A Universe of Desire

In the cosmos, a wish floats free,
A chocolate chip cookie just for me.
Planets made of candy, stars of pie,
Flying on marshmallows, oh my, oh my!

A comet whizzes by with a wink,
In this universe, I can finally think.
A rocket of giggles zooms with glee,
Let's launch into fun, just you and me.

Navigating by Starlight

With a map of giggles and stars to steer,
We sail through night skies, never fear.
Directions given by a wise old frog,
Who croaks out the path, though it's all a fog.

The moon is a disco ball, twinkling bright,
Calling us to dance in the cool moonlight.
Wandering whimsically, we float on dreams,
Life's a joke, or so it seems.

Pathways of the Imagination

In a forest of thought where squirrels can rhyme,
I wander pathways that bend and climb.
A talking tree whispers, 'Join the fun!'
In a world where logic has come undone.

Bubblegum bridges and clouds made of cheese,
Make me chuckle and feel at ease.
Each step a giggle, every turn a jest,
In this imaginative place, I feel blessed.

Journey of Dreams

In pajamas, I plot my grand trip,
With snacks piled high, just one little sip,
I'll sail on a couch, through the stars I will roam,
With video snacks, I'm feeling at home.

A map made of pizza, I'll chart my own course,
With pepperoni insights, I'll never feel worse,
Pajama-clad captain of this sweet ship,
In the ocean of Netflix, I take another dip.

Each nap is a stop, each dream is a quest,
"Did I win the lottery?" Nope, just some rest,
I'll conquer the world with my pillow so brave,
Fighting off worries with my cozy wave.

So here's to the dreamers, in slippers we stand,
Cherishing moments, both silly and grand,
With a wink and a giggle, we chase down our fun,
For the journey of dreams has only begun.

The Canvas of Existence

Life's a canvas, splattered in hues,
With crayons that melt, I pen my own views,
A painting of chaos, a splash of delight,
Who needs a straight line? I'll wing it tonight.

With chocolate for brown and candy for green,
Every stroke's a story, every dab's a scene,
I'm the artist of giggles, a master of joy,
My brush is my spoon, I don't need a ploy.

I daub on some chaos, and sprinkle in glee,
This masterpiece shines—not perfect, but free,
Where laughter adds texture, and silliness flows,
Who made the rules? Well, nobody knows!

So raise up your brushes, dear friends, let's paint,
With all of our quirks and our laughs that don't faint,
For a canvas of moments, we splash and we cheer,
In the gallery of fun, I'll see you right here!

Chasing Horizons

I chase after horizons on my bright, pink bike,
With a basket of cookies, oh what a delight,
Each pedal a giggle, each bump a small dance,
Who knew that the journey could give me a chance?

Waving at clouds, I laugh at the sun,
With a wink to the moon, my day's just begun,
From playground to park, I'm drawn like a spark,
My dreams are like bubbles, they pop in the dark.

I'll skip with a purpose, and trip with a grin,
Every tumble a dance, let the fun times begin,
With friends all around, we're a wild, crazy crew,
Chasing horizons with a side of gooey stew.

So hop on your bike, let's ride into cheer,
We'll chase down the laughter without any fear,
With a twist and a turn, some mischief in tow,
In the chase for horizons, we'll steal the show!

Echoes of Desire

In the depths of my fridge, I hear whispers so sweet,
"Last slice of pizza, come on, let's meet!"
I ponder my needs, oh the cravings arise,
The echoes of snacks are my ultimate prize.

With chips on my shirt, I dance in delight,
Each crunch is a giggle, each bite pure insight,
The fridge is a treasure, a buffet of dreams,
I'm the king of desire, or so it seems.

So let's toast to our wishes, both outrageous and grand,
With fudge and some sprinkles, we'll take a strong stand,
In this echoing kitchen, we laugh and we play,
With a feast for the senses, we'll party all day.

So come join the echoes, let's feast with some flair,
With a scoop of adventure and stories to share,
In the banquet of want, let's fill up our cheer,
For desires are funny, and laughter's the gear!

Beyond the Stars

In a galaxy of dreams, I play,

Dancing on comets, hip-hip-hooray!
Every wish has a twinkle, every laugh a beam,
Chasing my goals, like ice cream in a dream.

Aliens with hula-hoops make me grin,
Their space disco lights spark up my chin.
Floating past planets, in bubblegum shoes,
Who knew the cosmos had such fun news?

Galactic pets wag their tails with delight,
Even black holes can twirl when they feel light.
Mars throws a party, and Jupiter's jolly,
When it comes to the stars, you can't say sorry!

So here I zoom, with a heart full of glee,
Painting the night with my whimsy spree.
Explore the unknown, let imagination flow,
To the ends of the universe, I'm ready to go!

A Symphony of Wishes

Grab your kazoo, it's time to sing,

With rainbow confetti, let the joy spring.
Each wish a note in our quirky song,
Together we laugh, where we all belong.

A tuba of dreams and a flute of fun,
Playing all day till the setting sun.
Unicorns prance to our silly beat,
While dancing dinosaurs tap their feet.

Amid notes of hope, we skip with flair,
Making wishes fly high in the air.
With each silly giggle, a wish comes true,
What a symphony, just me and you!

So join the orchestra, let spirits rise,
Tune in to the magic that fills the skies.
With laughter as our guide and music our key,
Together we'll make the world wild and free!

The Dance of Possibilities

Put on your shoes, the floor is clear,

Let's twirl and spin, spread that cheer.
Every step a chance, every leap a call,
In the dance of life, we can have a ball.

Mismatched socks and polka dot ties,
Awkward twirls and exaggerated sighs.
Each dip and dive, a new path unfolds,
Moving to stories that life itself holds.

Even if you trip on your two left feet,
Just laugh it off, it's part of the beat.
Waltzing with wishes, a cha-cha of dreams,
Silly pirouettes bursting at the seams.

So grab a partner, or dance solo too,
In this grand ballroom, it's all up to you.
The rhythm of hopes will always align,
You're a star on this stage, so let yourself shine!

Colors of the Heart

With crayons in hand, I scribble away,

Painting my wishes in vibrant, bold array.
A splash of silly and a dash of bright,
Creating my canvas, a whimsical sight.

Yellow is laughter, and green is a spree,
Blue is the calm, wild thoughts set free.
Red's for the quirks, the fun times and cheer,
Each stroke tells a story, loud and clear.

Mixing it up like a crazy old chef,
Gifting my heart a colorful heft.
Wishing for giggles, while dodging the frowns,
Creating a masterpiece, in the world's clown towns.

So let's paint the world with glitter and glee,
Fill it with colors of what we can be.
Splash on the magic, one brush at a time,
In this universe's gallery, a life so sublime!

The Symphony of Us

In a world where socks might stray,
We dance to rhythms every day.
With spoons as instruments, we create,
A symphony of laughter, isn't that great?

Chasing dreams like cats in the night,
With each unexpected bump, we take flight.
We jump on clouds and slide on rain,
Mixing joy and quirks—a playful gain.

Oh, let's tickle the stars on a swing,
While eating candy, we'll wear a ring.
In this orchestra, we all belong,
Composing a tune, singing our song.

We'll jive on marshmallows, jump on pies,
With silly giggles and sweet surprise.
Through weird adventures, we find the keys,
To a wacky vibe that never frees.

The Mirror's Truth

Look in the glass—oh what a face,
A quirky grin, lacking grace.
Reflections play tricks, oh what fun,
Like chasing shadows, one by one.

I polish my ego, ask for a wink,
In this world, we all overthink.
A mirror laughs back, don't take it too harsh,
Just remember, everyone's on this march.

Twirling around in pajamas at noon,
Believing hard in a cartoon moon.
With every glance, I find the lore,
Of silly quirks I simply adore.

So hold on tight to your own quirks,
For in them lie the finest perks.
From every giggle to every gaffe,
Life's just a punchline—a joyful laugh!

Horizons of the Infinite

In a land of endless cheese and bread,
We'll sail on noodles, and not on spread.
Across the seas of jelly beans,
We'll hunt for rainbows, oh, what scenes!

With capes of paper, we'll take flight,
Dancing on clouds, with sheer delight.
Every step and jump, a brand new tune,
Under the glow of a candy moon.

Exploring lands where the shadows play,
Imagining a silly, goofy day.
Each twist and turn, a laugh parade,
In this grand journey, memories made.

So gather round, the world's a stage,
With gags and pranks, let's disengage.
For on this journey, fun is the goal,
As we chase horizons, both bright and whole.

A Journey Within

Deep inside, where giggles grow,
I find a treasure, more than I know.
With silly songs and playful grace,
Exploring the nooks of my own space.

A rollercoaster ride through thoughts and dreams,
Like chocolate rivers, or whipped cream streams.
Dancing with doubts, we share a laugh,
In quirky rooms of a curious path.

Let's play hide-and-seek with time,
While munching on cookies, oh so sublime.
With every glance into my heart,
A giggle erupts, a joyful start.

On this journey of fun and cheer,
We'll celebrate quirks, year after year.
For in these moments, wild and free,
I find the humor inside of me.

The Alchemy of Choices

Choices like socks, mismatched and bold,
Adventure awaits, or so I'm told.
Flip a coin, or take a chance,
Who knew my fate danced in a glance?

Pick a path, it's quite the ride,
Sometimes I trip, but I'm filled with pride.
A cookie crumbles, it speaks to me,
Will it be chocolate, or just plain brie?

Sauce or no sauce, just do what feels right,
Spaghetti or tacos, it's all in my sight.
I spin the wheel, I twirl and I sway,
Every wrong turn leads me to play.

So here's to the choices, wild and free,
I'll stake my claim in sheer jubilee.
Let life be the circus, I'll juggle with glee,
On this wacky ride, just come join me!

Manifesting Possibilities

I woke up dreaming, what shall I make?
A pancake that flips, or a giant cake?
Manifesting wishes, the list grows long,
Or maybe just dance, it can't be wrong!

A unicorn frolics, in a bubble bath,
While I scribble plans, and do the math.
To float like a cloud, or race a fast car,
Who knew ambition could spark such bizarre?

An army of ducks in my future parade,
I'll have them marching, no plans disobeyed.
Pies in the sky, or balloons filled with hope,
Every silly thought, helps me to cope.

So let's paint the world in colors so bright,
With whims and with wonders that bring pure delight.
What shall we conjure, just take a chance,
In this madcap universe, let us dance!

Portrait of the Future

In my crystal ball, I see silly sights,
Kittens in hats practicing heights.
A future so bright, it dazzles my eyes,
Wait, is that a pie that can talk and tell lies?

Next, it shows me, a dog doing yoga,
Prancing around in quite the euphoria.
His downward dog, such a sight to behold,
While cookie dough dreams, he treats as gold.

A robot chef that can't boil some rice,
But serves up laughs, which is quite nice.
I paint my portrait with silly extremes,
Every playful moment is woven with dreams.

So come take a peek at this canvas so strange,
Where every oddity dances and plays.
In the portrait of future, just let it be fun,
Turn your weird dreams into something you've won!

The Mirror of Aspirations

I looked in the mirror, what did I see?
A knight in pajamas, charging with glee.
My goals are balloons, floating up high,
With marshmallow dreams that tickle the sky.

A tale of a baker who burns every pie,
Yet, serves a feast that makes you ask why.
Aspire for laughter, it's easier to find,
When cupcakes are flying through the air, oh so kind.

A mirror reflecting a wild, wacky truth,
Where goals are just giggles, and joy is your proof.
Plant seeds of ambition, just watch them bloom,
In a garden of chaos, there's always room.

So let's toast to the future, in hats and in cake,
With every reflection, new paths we shall make.
Dance in the moment, let aspirations take flight,
For who needs a plan when you can just delight?

The Symphony of Choices

In the concert of decisions we play,
With each note, we stumble or sway,
Grab a trombone or a bright kazoo,
Life's a symphony, decked out in blue.

The conductor is quirky, a little offbeat,
Sometimes we march to the sound of our feet,
Singing high notes, or perhaps off-key,
In this wild orchestra, you just might see.

Pick your instrument, just don't get bored,
Bongos or bagpipes? It's your reward!
Swirl and twirl in this whimsical jam,
And know that you're wilder than any ol' clam.

So bring out the brass, let the woodwinds cheer,
With each giggle and chuckle, let's toast with a beer,
Our choices compose this hilarious score,
In this symphonic chaos, we always want more.

Dancing with Destiny

Twirl and spin, let fate take the lead,
In this wacky waltz, let your heart take heed,
Step on your toes? Oh, what a delight!
Just laugh it off, we're dancing all night!

With every misstep, we giggle and sigh,
Moonwalks and limbos, oh my oh my!
Salsa through troubles, cha-cha with glee,
In this silly dance, there's no need to flee.

Hold on to your partner, the floor's feeling hot,
We're dancing like mad, if you give it a shot,
A tango with dreams, a jig with the past,
Each twirl and each dip makes the moments last.

So let's shimmy and shake with a playful intent,
Sway with your dreams, and don't be lament!
In this dance of the quirky, the silly, the free,
We find our own steps and just let it be.

Unwritten Chapters

Pages await with blank, eager space,
Grab a pen, let's start this race!
Sketch out a dragon or a gremlin in flight,
Make each line silly, and keep it light!

Once there was a knight, or maybe a cat,
Frolicking forests while wearing a hat,
What's next on this journey? A bubblegum sea?
With each silly story, there's more to see!

Plot twists galore, don't follow the norm,
Maybe a storm? Or a chicken that's warm?
Add in some laughter, a sprinkle of fun,
We'll create a story that's just second to none.

So flip to the pages, the ink's ready now,
Write your adventure, take your own bow,
With each turn, let the craziness swell,
In the book of the quirky, all can dwell.

A Tapestry of Wishes

Threads of desire, all colors unite,
Weave them together, a fabulous sight!
A splash of blue for pizza and cake,
A pinch of pink for each silly mistake.

Stitch in some laughter, let joy intertwine,
With wacky ambitions, life's just divine,
Knots of connection, each wish a delight,
In this tapestry tangled, oh, what a sight!

Wrap up your dreams with a sequined flair,
Embroider your hopes; hang them with care,
Tuck in some giggles and a dash of fun,
In this fabric of wishes, we're never done!

So grab your yarn, let's get crafting today,
With each stitch, we celebrate play,
In this rainbow of dreams, so wild and so bright,
We'll quilt all our whims and dance through the night!

Cascading Dreams

In a world of jellybeans, I dream and scheme,
With unicorns as friends, so bright they gleam.
Chasing rainbows on my lunch break spree,
Life's a buffet, I'll take one of each for me!

Kites are flying high, they tickle the sky,
While I invent new ways to say goodbye.
Dance like no one sees, with socks on my feet,
Life's a circus, and I'm the clown with the beat!

A treasure map drawn in my pancake stack,
With syrup rivers leading on the right track.
Pirates of my breakfast, toast swords held high,
On a quest for jam, we'll conquer the sky!

So here's to the whims, the giggles, the glee,
For every wild thought brings a chance to be free.
So grab your paintbrush, let colors collide,
In the fairytale world where humor's the guide.

Strokes of Fate

A canvas of chaos, splashes galore,
Accidental masterpieces, who could ask for more?
With coffee as my muse, I throw caution aside,
Dancing with brushes, my sanity is fried!

Mistakes are my friends, we paint on a spree,
Each bobble and blunder is a party for me.
A squirrel in my hat, it's just how I roll,
In the gallery of giggles, I'm the star of the soul!

The sun wears sunglasses, moon's trying to cheer,
Clouds throw a confetti storm, just to draw near.
In this wild exhibit where laughter's the norm,
Brush strokes of fate create a colorful storm.

So swirl with the chaos, embrace every hue,
Masterpieces await in the world made for you.
With every mad scribble, let joy take the lead,
In the realm of tomfoolery, we all plant a seed.

The Essence of Longing

I long for that pizza with extra cheese bliss,
With toppings galore, it's a culinary kiss.
Dough tossing dreams, I'm the chef on the quest,
To find the perfect slice, I'm on a taste test!

Chasing after cupcakes that dance on the street,
While donuts roll by to the rhythm of beat.
In a land made of sweets, I'd like to reside,
With marshmallow clouds, where I frolic and glide!

Underneath the sprinkles, I'll search for the prize,
A fountain of chocolate, oh what a surprise!
With gummy bear pals doing splits with great flair,
In the land of my longings, there's nothing but care.

So let's celebrate wishes with frolic and fun,
Finding joy in the little things, we're never outdone.
With teaspoons of laughter, and a sprinkle of cheer,
In the essence of longing, we'll always be near.

The Artwork of Your Days

Brush strokes of giggles paint the morning bright,
   With sunbeams as glitter, oh what a sight!
   Doodles of dreams on the canvas of play,
   With zany adventures coloring up the day!

A whimsical waltz with the clock on my wall,
   It tickles and tocks, making nonsense its call.
   I sketch out my moments with flair and pizzazz,
   In the gallery of chaos, my style is the jazz!

With ice cream as clouds, and sprinkles for trees,
The landscape of laughter flows soft in the breeze.
   So grab your wild palette and let colors sing,
For the artwork of your days is a marvelous thing!

Each mishap, each giggle, each clumsy parade,
Makes your tapestry richer, with every charade.
   In a gallery of whimsy, you hold the best brush,
   Creating your masterpiece, never in a rush!

Whispers in the Wind

In the breeze, I hear a shout,
"Pick a path, figure it out!"
A squirrel scurries with a glance,
It seems to know how to prance.

Though options swirl like autumn leaves,
The cat just naps under the eaves.
I grab my coffee, sip, then nod,
While pigeons plot their next facade.

Should I dance or take a jog?
Join the circus or walk the dog?
Each day's a fun surprise, you'll see,
As I chase my dreams like a bumblebee.

So here's the twist, enjoy the ride,
With snacks and laughs, I won't hide.
For in the end, it's clear to see,
The purpose is just being me!

A Thread of Choices

I wake each morn, toss dice for fun,
Should I play or should I run?
A slice of toast or pancakes tall?
My breakfast game can't be too small.

A juggler's fate or a poet's peace,
From every choice, my worries cease.
With laughter bright, I spin my thread,
Who knows where this whimsy will be led?

Maybe I'll learn to bake a cake,
Or just binge-watch a brand new fake.
With friends and jokes, I sprout my wings,
And in this dance, the happiness rings.

So let's embrace this wacky wheel,
Where choices swirl, that's the deal!
Tomorrow's folly is just a tease,
But today, that sounds like a breeze!

Embracing the Unknown

Peeking out from cozy beds,
What awaits? I scratch my head.
The fridge hums songs of secret meals,
But I crave the thrill of wobbly wheels.

Trying new things can make you frown,
Like wearing socks that tumble down.
Yet laughter bubbles in the fray,
As I stumble through my goofy play.

A wild dance with a cactus there,
Or serenading in my underwear.
The unknown is a topped-up cone,
Sprinkled with zest, it's all my own!

So bring on life with all its quirks,
I'll ride the waves and play with jerks.
For each bizarre twist and bend I take,
Is just another laugh, for joy's own sake!

The Rhythm of Ambitions

Dreams like shoes in tangled laces,
Each step a dance in funny places.
With every stumble, giggles rise,
As I power through with wide-eyed sighs.

Should I climb or fly on broom,
Is that a goal or just a zoom?
The rhythm plays a merry tune,
As I plan to juggle with a balloon.

With silly hats and polka dots,
I chase ambitions, not the plots.
With lemonade and endless cheer,
My silly heart has no need to steer.

So sway along to this quirky beat,
Where every choice is oh-so-sweet.
For in this dance, both wild and free,
The best ambition's just to be me!

A Universe Yet to Bloom

In the morning, I sip my brew,
Dreams of grandeur, just a few.
A cat on a couch, a dog on a stool,
World domination? Nah, just play the fool.

Lost in a maze of pancake stacks,
Wearing socks that don't match, facts!
My life's a circus, complete with clown,
But hey, no need to frown, just goof around!

Stars in the sky, I aim to reach,
But I often get lost when I go to the beach.
A sunburned nose brings the laughter loud,
As I strut like a peacock, feeling so proud.

So grab your dreams, toss them high,
Like a kite that wants just to fly.
In this universe, let giggles reign,
And find joy in every silly gain!

The Heart's Odyssey

With a heart that dances, spins, and twirls,
I chase my dreams like a kid with pearls.
Tickle my fancy, make me grin,
Adventure awaits, where to begin?

Eating cake while dressed like a knight,
In a quest for the fridge, a hilarious sight.
Goblins of laundry block my way,
But crumbs are my treasure, I'll barge, hooray!

I ponder deep beneath the sky,
While plotting just how to fly.
Balancing whimsy with a cup of tea,
Oh, the places I'll go—just wait and see!

With jest and folly, I ride the tide,
On the waves of laughter, I take pride.
In a world that spins, full of delight,
Let's dance through the chaos, from day to night!

Heartbeats of Ambition

In a world of jellybeans and dreams,
I chase my goals like ice cream themes.
With a spoon in hand, I dig right in,
Who knew success could taste like tin?

I craft my plans with duct tape and hope,
Riding my dreams like a wobbly slope.
Falling forward, landing on my face,
But laughter is my favorite embrace.

Every stumble is a dance I do,
Salsa steps on a floor of blue.
With each little whim, I flip and twirl,
Dancing with fortune, watch me unfurl.

So here's to the joys and silly blunders,
To dreams that sparkle like cosmic wonders.
With a grin, I'll chase and I'll swing,
Finding laughter in every little thing.

Weaving Tomorrow

With yarn of colors bright and bold,
I knit my future, or so I'm told.
Some stitches drop, but I just restart,
Creating a tapestry of silly art.

I measure moments in cups of tea,
Adding sugar for sweet clarity.
Crochet hooks dance in a merry sway,
Twisting time into a funny display.

Spools of dreams on a spinning wheel,
Each turn brings a giggle appeal.
With threads of joy and knots of bliss,
I weave my path with a cheeky kiss.

In a patchwork quilt of hope and cheer,
I patch up woes with laughter and beer.
So here's to tomorrow, a playful sight,
Bringing joy to the stitches of delight.

The Garden of Intentions

In a garden where wishes bloom and thrive,
I plant my dreams, hoping they'll arrive.
With watering cans filled with delight,
I sprinkle laugh tracks on seeds of light.

Weeds of worry try to take their place,
But I hoe them down with a funny face.
With gnome companions, they guide my way,
In a dance with daisies, come what may.

Sunshine beams like a vibrant grin,
Photosynthesizing all that's within.
Each blossom laughs in colors so jolly,
As I skip through rows with a melody folly.

So come wander through this quirky patch,
Where aspirations grow without a scratch.
In blooms of joy, let's take a stand,
Harvesting giggles, hand in hand.

The Heart's Navigation

My heart's a sailor in an ocean wide,
With a compass that spins, I take my ride.
Charting maps on the back of my hand,
Navigating whims like a soft, sappy band.

With a parrot named Dreamy on my shoulder,
We shout at the waves, growing bolder.
"Set sail for laughter!" I boldly proclaim,
As we dance with the tides of whimsical fame.

Oh, the stars are guides in the night sky,
Twinkling gems as we howl and sigh.
Sailing through clouds shaped like cats,
With our noses in the breeze, wearing funny hats.

So raise your glasses to adventures bright,
To hearts that wander in playful flight.
With sails unfurled in hilarious glee,
I'll find my way, wherever that may be.

Stars in Your Hands

You reach for the sky, a star in your grip,
But it's really just candy, a sweet little trip.
With sprinkles of laughter and giggles galore,
Just be careful, my friend, it's a sticky explore.

You dream of a comet, a rocket to ride,
Yet find yourself tripping, arms flailing wide.
Just remember to laugh, it's all a good jest,
Stars are for dreaming, but snacks are the best.

In your hands are the wishes, the joys of the night,
But don't drop your ice cream; that's a sad sight!
With each little twinkle, let your heart take a dance,
Life's just a circus, so give it a chance.

So twirl in the starlight, with glitter and cheer,
Pluck random wishes, or maybe a beer!
For in this wide universe, you're silly and grand,
Just remember, dear friend, you have stars in your hand.

The Art of Becoming

Once I was nothing, a speck on the floor,
Now I'm a masterpiece, a walking decor.
With mismatched socks and a smile on my face,
I'm evolving each day, at my own crazy pace.

I tried to be serious, a corporate chap,
But ended up rolling in a big ol' nap.
Sipping on dreams with a side of delight,
I'm the artist of life, painting joy day and night.

With brushes of laughter and shades of pure fun,
I mix all my chaos; the canvas is done.
From crayons to chaos, I let my heart lead,
In the gallery of living, I'm just planting my seed.

So here's to the changes, the quirks that we flaunt,
In the grand art of becoming, it's joy that we haunt!
So grab your bright colors, and let laughter's bell ring,
For our journey is wild, it's the best kind of fling.

Journey of a Thousand Yesterdays

I wandered through yesterday, lost in the past,
Chasing my shadows, they move way too fast.
I laughed at my blunders, each tumble and fall,
Turns out this 'journey' is a circus of sprawl.

Each step that I take, I try not to trip,
But hey, every stumble's a free little slip!
I collected my failures like stamps in a book,
For giggles and chuckles, life knows how to cook.

From hiccups of laughter to blunders sublime,
My yesterdays dance like they're free-drunk on rhyme.
With folly and fun, I spin round the sun,
Just call me a comet, too wild to outrun.

So here's to the past, with its winks and its smirks,
Each nuance like glitter that endlessly lurks.
I'm weaving a future from threads of my laughs,
In the journey of being, let's take all the gaffes!

Ink on an Open Page

With ink on my fingers, I scribble some dreams,
Like coffee-stained pages, bursting at the seams.
Each word is a giggle, a wink and a tease,
As I write out my story, simply done with ease.

Every line is a dance, a cha-cha of thought,
With metaphors jumping, and similes fought.
I pen down my nonsense in bubbles and puns,
For laughter is magic, and my heart always runs.

In the margins, I doodle, my mind's little spree,
With unicorns prancing, all wild and carefree.
I'm spilling my soul on this canvas so grand,
With ink on my fingers and joy at command.

So here's to the scribbles, the giggles we chase,
To letters and stories, a wild, happy place.
With each little squiggle, my heart starts to sing,
In the realm of my pages, I'll dance like a king.

Unraveled Journeys

I packed my bags, set out to roam,
But forgot half my snacks, I miss my home.
The map was upside down, oh what a tease,
I ended up grillin' squirrels and cheese.

With every turn, a new surprise,
A talking dog with googly eyes!
He told me jokes, made me laugh like mad,
Turns out my journey ain't so bad.

A rainbow bridge? I tripped and fell,
Landed in a pond, what a funny smell!
Fish giggled, I splashed, "I'm the new queen!"
But the frogs croaked back, "Honey, you mean 'bean'!"

So off I go, no plan in sight,
Chasing unicorns and green delight.
With every misstep, I learn and play,
Who knew adventures could be this cray?

The Dance of Serendipity

Bumped into fate, stepped on a toe,
Tripped on my dreams, with a stellar show.
A twist of the wrist, a whirl and a twirl,
Caught in a jest with a dancing squirrel.

A disco ball hung from a rainbow tree,
Where moles in tuxedos danced with glee.
They offered me snacks, "Come join the fun!"
My snacks could wait; this shindig's begun.

We shimmy and shake, with polka-dot flair,
With a playlist crafted by a grizzly bear.
Jellybeans fall like confetti from skies,
And laughter erupts, oh what a surprise!

As the music fades, I wave goodbye,
To my furry friends under the peachy sky.
The dance of the day, a frothy delight,
In the rhythm of chaos, everything's right!

Chords of the Future

Plucked a string on my ukulele bright,
Created a tune that took off in flight.
Each note I strummed, the world went wild,
Even the cats joined, they purred and smiled.

A frog on a log dropped a sick beat,
With a tap-dancing turtle, oh so neat!
The sun joined in with a shining grin,
As I crooned about spaghetti and sin.

In this jam session of the zany crew,
A snail in shades said, "I'll sing too!"
With a voice like honey, he stole the show,
While ants brought the rhythm, stealing the flow.

What's next in this symphony of fun?
A squirrel with a tambourine, on the run!
Each strum and each laugh becomes the way,
To create a future that's wacky and gay!

Beyond the Veil

I peeked behind curtains of mystery bright,
To find Granny ghosting, just shooting the light.
"Remember to dance!" she said with a wink,
"Life's too short, kiddo! Go grab a drink!"

In a jiffy, we spun through cosmic soup,
Dodging strange creatures in a vibrant loop.
A hipster goblin offered me brew,
With flavors so wild, I thought, "What's this, stew?"

Floating through portals with sparkles galore,
Met a witty elf who stole my shoe store.
"With one in your hand, you're still part of the game!"
I laughed till I cried; nothing was the same!

So remember the tales from beyond our sight,
With bumbles and giggles, let all feel right.
Embrace what comes next, be silly, be bold,
For beyond every veil, is a story untold!

Rivers of Reflection

I stared into a puddle, oh so bright,
Thought about my future, what a sight!
Should I be a chef or maybe a clown?
Dancing while flipping pancakes upside down!

A fish swam by, gave me a wink,
"Choose popcorn over fate!" it did think.
So here I am, with butter and zest,
Life is a snack, and I'm just the best!

The birds overhead giggle and peep,
As I leap about, dreams not so cheap.
A river of giggles flows deep and wide,
With every belly laugh, I take a ride!

So splash in your dreams, do not delay,
Life's just a buffet; come, serve it your way!
Wear that big hat and dance like a king,
In this grand carnival, let your heart sing!

Tides of the Heart

At twilight, the waves tickled my toes,
What shall I be? A gardener or prose?
The sea whispers secrets, salty and sweet,
Maybe I'll surf on a wave of retreat.

A crab scuttles past with a curious blink,
"Find your own rhythm, don't overthink!"
So I twirl like a seaweed, flapping about,
Chasing the seagulls with a well-timed shout!

The sandcastles crumble, and so do my fears,
Laughter erupts; we'll need more than tears.
With each ebb and flow, there's freedom in mess,
Paint your grin wide; it's your own kind of dress!

And when the tide pulls, don't mind the fate,
Dance with the moon; celebrate what's great!
In this funny ocean, let's ride every wave,
For surfs up at twilight; it's us who'll be brave!

The Journey Curved

On a winding road with snacks by my side,
I ponder my journeys, and where to reside.
Should I climb a mountain or nap in a field?
Career as a snail? That option's revealed!

Each turn is a giggle, each bump a delighted squeak,
As I zigzag my path, I stumble, lose streak.
A squirrel gives chase, or perhaps it's a race,
Life on this journey is full of fun pace!

The GPS reboots, makes up its own laws,
"Turn left at the laughter, right at the applause!"
So off I go, twirling, with no real plan,
Maybe an astronaut, or just a fan!

The maps can be silly, but oh, they excite!
Join in the jest, let's laugh through the night.
Dear travelers, hold tight with whimsy and cheer,
Every twist is a chance; for joy, we steer!

A Symphony of Strivings

I play the piano with socks on my hands,
Each note a giggle, each chord a handful of sands.
Musical chairs in a world made of dreams,
Where breakfast for dinner is bursting at the seams!

The trumpet's a cat, it meows out loud,
While violins dance with a playful crowd.
A symphony? More like a carnival play,
With laughter as lyrics, let's party away!

I've dreamed of the stage, of bright flashing lights,
But I'm in my pajamas, feeling so light.
To be or not to be? Let's skip that old line,
In this melodic chaos, we sip on good wine!

So join in the chorus, take heart in your sway,
Each strum is a whimsy; let's laugh through the day.
With a symphony of strivings, we twirl and we weave,
In this wild little tune, there's magic to believe!

Embracing the Unknown

In a land where choices sprout,
I stood confused, filled with doubt.
A pie chart of dreams, one slice to eat,
But then I decided, life's really sweet.

With every turn, a quirky twist,
Like dancing with socks, can't resist.
Spotting a cat wearing a hat,
I chuckled, and thought, 'Well, how about that!'

Each path I take, a new delight,
A game of chess in the dead of night.
I've got a plan, or maybe not,
Just follow the cake – well, that's my plot!

So here's to chaos, cheers to the whim,
A buffet of choices—more, not less grim.
Juggling the jeery with blissful cheer,
I leap into life—hold my juice, dear!

The Quest of the Self

I set off on a quest so grand,
With a map made mostly of quicksand.
Searching for wisdom in the fridge,
Maybe some yogurt can bridge that ridge.

I met a wise owl—well, a plush toy,
"Find yourself!" it hooted with joy.
I pondered deeply, scratched my head,
Then realized—he was just well-fed.

In the mirror, I faced a zany sight,
A funky hairdo, what a fright!
But laughter erupted—it couldn't be worse,
Who knew self-love was a comical curse?

So off I ventured, untamed and bold,
Chasing my dreams, or at least, some gold.
Every absurd step, I embraced with glee,
In this whimsical journey, I found me!

Sailor of Dreams

A sailor set out on a banana boat,
Waving goodbye to a quirky goat.
With a compass spinning, it called him near,
"Let's sail for cheese—with no need for fear!"

Through jellyfish seas and clouds of fluff,
His heart was light, the waves—just tough.
A treasure map drawn in crayon and mess,
"Follow your nose, that's how you'll impress!"

With every wave, a belly flop,
He laughed and danced, "Oh, I can't stop!"
The horizon promised pies on display,
"Why not just eat all on the way?"

So here he drifts, not lost but found,
On cotton candy waves, joy unbound.
Life's a treasure—whatever it seems,
Set sail, my friend, you're a sailor of dreams!

The Rhythm of Possibilities

In a world of beats and twirling spins,
I danced on shoes made of thickened fins.
With every step, a giggle would rise,
As I juggled wishes beneath sunny skies.

The melody played, oh so absurd,
A tune that only the chickens heard.
Twisting and diving, no time to fret,
Mixing it up, no need for regret!

Skipping along with a side-stepping cat,
We both sang loudly, 'How about that?'
In the rhythm of life, each chance a chance,
Even the stumbles can lead to a dance!

So grab a hat, let's sing off-key,
In this dance of moments, you and me.
The symphony swirls, wild and free,
Embrace each note; let your spirit agree!

The Journey Within

In search of meaning, here I roam,
Chasing my thoughts, far from home.
Each twist and turn, a laugh or two,
Who knew my sock had dreams? Did you?

With a map that's scribbled, upside down,
I trip on hopes, then wear a frown.
A bird just mocked my three-course meal,
Turns out, it's just a breakfast peel.

The bus of wishes, it missed my stop,
But hey, there's ice cream at the top!
I'll climb up high on a mountain of 'meh,'
Finding joy in all the quirky banter, hey?

So here I wheel, my mind a fair,
Where every thought just stops to stare.
And though the journey's never straight,
It's snacks and giggles that truly await.

Echoes of Your Voice

In a world where echoes play,
Whispers dance, come what may.
I asked a quokka, 'Am I okay?'
It laughed and said, 'Just seize the day!'

Voices drift like cotton candy,
They bounce and twirl, isn't that handy?
One shouted, 'You've got two left feet!'
I responded, 'Well, at least they're sweet!'

In this circus of opinions loud,
I might just wear a zany shroud.
A lion roars, but a frog just croaks,
While I juggle life like silly jokes.

So let your echoes paint the sky,
With laughter bright, oh my, oh my!
Whether whispered soft or shouted bold,
Each voice is magic, watch it unfold.

Dreams Alight

I lit a match to spark a dream,
It flickered once, then shed a beam.
Thought it'd burst like Fourth of July,
But instead, it fizzled—oh my, oh my!

The toaster popped, a dream too dark,
Burnt offerings, like a cruel remark.
Yet dreams can dance on buttered bread,
With each bite, new flavors spread.

I tied balloons to hopes in flight,
They floated up, then laughed with fright.
A cat walked by, with a look so sly,
'You'll never catch me,' it seemed to cry.

But still I chase, this merry game,
With every stumble, there's joy to claim.
For dreams, you see, are not a race,
But rather a dance, like pie in your face!

The Mosaic of Identity

A patchwork quilt of I and me,
Stitching together who I can be.
One square's an avocado toast delight,
While another's a sock that's taken flight.

I wear my quirks like a badge, you know,
From mismatched shoes to a bright yellow bow.
The mirror laughs, 'Oh look at that!'
Reflections that wave like a quirky hat.

I'm part superhero, part goofball queen,
My cape? Why yes, it's glittering green!
With every piece, I'm more alive,
Creating a mix that will surely thrive.

So here's to the jigsaw, each piece in sight,
Embracing the mess and feeling just right.
For in this mosaic, my heart's set free,
I'm all that I am, and laugh with glee!

Seeds of Tomorrow

In the garden of dreams, we scatter the seeds,
Water them with laughter, fulfill our wild needs.
Some grow into pumpkins, others just weeds,
But hey, even weeds can sprout funny creeds.

Planting ambitions, a quirky delight,
One's aiming for stardust, another for bite.
Chasing the clouds while catching the light,
Mixing dreams with realities, oh what a sight!

We harvest confusion, jar it with cheer,
Planting the bizarre, season after year.
Dancing with nonsense, a whimsical tier,
The plot thickens daily, our purpose sincere.

So come join the circus, we all have a role,
Be the jester or magician, play the card you stole.
In this garden of fun, let the small things console,
For every odd seed has a story to unroll.

Uncharted Paths

With a wink and a nudge, I wander away,
Search for the path that leads me to play.
Twists and turns, like a game of charades,
Sometimes I lose sight, but hey, it's okay!

Maps are for boring, just give me the thrill,
Forget all the rules, let's bend time at will.
I'll dance with the squirrels and climb up the hill,
Turning stones into gold, or so I feel.

A detour through donuts, a pause for some fries,
Every corner's a chance for delightful surprise.
Rollercoaster dreams and balloon-filled skies,
The journey's the giggle; I'll savor the highs.

So strap on your sneakers, let's skip to our tune,
Sing to the stars and dance with the moon.
Life's a big cookout; we'll feast as we swoon,
With uncharted paths, we're never marooned!

Destiny in Motion

We're all just marionettes on strings of delight,
Bouncing through life like a kite in mid-flight.
Twisting our fates like a pretzel not right,
Giggling at moments that give us a fright.

Every misstep's a dance, every stumble, a prance,
Shuffling through chaos, embracing the chance.
With a chuckle and grin, we enter the dance,
In this wacky parade, we all take a stance.

The universe chuckles, handing us beans,
Planting our laughter in whimsical scenes.
We march with our quirks, the oddest of dreams,
Finding our rhythm in silly routines.

So let's strut our stuff, no map in our hand,
A comedy show, isn't it grand?
With destiny spinning, let's take a stand,
In the theater of life, let's create our own band!

The Alchemy of Aspirations

Mixing up wishes in a cauldron of cheer,
Stirring up giggles as we spread out the gear.
Dreams bubble and froth, all deliciously queer,
The potion of hopes, let's toast with a beer!

Sprinkle in some nonsense, add a dash of zing,
The recipe's silly, with a side of bling.
Flip-flops are armor; we'll fashion a king,
Inventing our triumphs, let's see what they bring!

Alchemy of wishes, so brightly we shine,
Transforming our hiccups into jewels divine.
With laughter as currency, we trade to align,
In this world of opportunities, let's sip like fine wine.

So gather your dreams, let them dance in the light,
In this raucous adventure, we all take flight.
The alchemy's magic, it feels just so right,
With giggles and joy, we'll soar through the night!

Navigating the Labyrinth

In a maze of socks, I roam,
Searching for that perfect comb.
Each corner turned, a snack appears,
I laugh alone, but who needs peers?

Maps of spaghetti line my wall,
With cheese as currency, I stand tall.
The exit's near, or maybe not,
I'll just sit here—who needs a spot?

A treasure hunt for missing shoes,
Wandering wrong, I find the blues.
But with every twist, a chip I munch,
This labyrinth's a perfect lunch!

So here I wander, lost in glee,
Happy to be just me, not free.
For in this maze, I find my song,
With silly steps, I'll dance along!

The Mosaic of Intent

Broken tiles upon the floor,
Each piece tells a tale of yore.
With ketchup stains and coffee rings,
My mosaic sings of little things.

I set a goal to bake a pie,
But ended up with pudding dry.
Yet somehow lived to tell the tale,
Of how my dessert became a fail.

With crayons bright, I plan my dreams,
But scribbles end up bursting seams.
Each little mess, a quirky spark,
In this grand scheme, I leave my mark.

So gather scraps, embrace the flaws,
Each jumbled thought a round of applause.
For in this chaos, joy is found,
A patchwork life, colorful and sound!

Shadows and Silhouettes

In the corners, shadows dance,
With silly moves, they take a chance.
They trip and fall, a comical show,
In the sunlight's glow, they steal the show.

My silhouette's a funny sight,
With arms that wave and legs that might.
I stretch and yawn, they mock my pose,
In this shadow duel, who really knows?

Yet when the day bids night farewell,
The shadows laugh, they know me well.
They twist and twirl, a playful jest,
A partner to my daytime quest.

When darkness falls, I let them lead,
As my quiet dreams begin to seed.
With giggles shared under the moon,
We dance till dawn, a silly tune!

Tapestry of the Self

Threads of gold and bright fuzz balls,
I weave my tale in little squalls.
With mismatched styles and bright designs,
Each stitch a laugh, a world intertwines.

A knot here ties a joyful fall,
A loose thread, a spontaneous call.
Embroidered hopes in colors wild,
My quirky heart forever a child.

In patterns strange and knots so tight,
I dance with fabric, day and night.
For what's a tapestry if not a jest?
A patchwork quilt of perfect zest!

So let it fray, let colors bleed,
Each thread a joy, a tiny seed.
In this grand craft, I find my way,
With stitches sewn in bright array!

The Pioneer's Quest

In a land full of snacks, I did roam,
Chasing dreams made of cheese, oh, how they foam.
I mapped out my journey with ketchup and fries,
But missed the detour – that led to the pies.

Each step was a dance, a hop and a skip,
With marshmallow clouds, I'd take a big dip.
I built a fine castle with crumbs from my lunch,
Labeled it "Success" – then I ate it for brunch.

So here's to the trails paved with candy and cream,
Where nothing is silly and all's just a dream.
I climbed up a mountain of pickle and cheese,
And laughed at the thought of conveying my ease.

The moral is clear, or is it just jumbled?
In this quest for a purpose, I often have stumbled.
Just look for the laughs, they'll lead you ahead,
Together with snacks, there's nothing to dread!

Flames of Determination

I lit up a fire with my hopes and my bold,
But ended up grilling my dreams in the cold.
S'mores on the side, I laughed at the plight,
Determined to dance 'til the morning's first light.

With marshmallows toasted, and chocolate in hand,
I pondered my greatness, where dreams go to land.
My vision was clear as a ketchup-stained glass,
But yeah, I forgot – I can't light it with sass!

So fuel up the flames with a pinch of mad glee,
And watch as those dreams bounce around wildly!
Each flicker, each spark, a giggle along,
While figuring out where the heck I belong.

But never fear friends, I'm not lost at sea,
Still charting my course, with some gumballs for free.
With laughter in hand and a fork in my quest,
The warmth of my heart knows this madness is best!

The Chisel of Choice

With a chisel in hand, I began to create,
A statue of purpose, oh what a strange fate!
Each block that I chipped off was shaped like a shoe,
But somehow it turned into a pet kangaroo.

As I carved out a vision, it wobbled and squeaked,
I giggled aloud, for it talked back and peeked.
My choices, it seemed, were as odd as a sock,
But why follow norms when you can paint a flock?

So I sculpted my destiny in colors so bright,
With each silly choice, I danced through the night.
In the end, it's clear, we're all a bit cracked,
But humor and joy keep our spirits unpacked.

So grab your own chisel, make choices galore,
And don't fret or worry if they create folklore.
For the quirkiest shapes are the ones that we find,
Let's mold out our futures with a happy mind!

Embracing Every Chapter

In a book full of giggles, I turn every page,
With plots filled with jellybeans and taffy for wage.
Each chapter a twist of the silliest plot,
Where cats wear top hats and dance on the spot.

With a grin and a chuckle, I delve into tales,
Of penguins on scooters, and llamas with sails.
Each laugh brings me closer to what I can be,
A wizard, a pirate, perhaps even a bee!

So I wobble through stories, both funny and wild,
Finding joy in each journey, like a carefree child.
For life is a book, let's write it with glee,
Where every strange chapter is the best one for me.

So gather 'round, friends, let's flip through the fun,
With rubber bands, unicorns – together we run.
In pages of laughter, may we always find rest,
Embracing each chapter, for humor is best!

The Path of Your Making

Wake up with a grin, decide it's your day,
Socks that don't match? That's totally okay!
Chase after a dream, or maybe a snack,
The map's just a doodle, so cut yourself slack.

Pick purple or yellow, like stars on a whim,
The road might be bumpy, but don't let it dim.
A dance with your cat, or a jog in the rain,
Turn frowns into giggles, erase every pain.

Grab your creaky scooter or an old pogo stick,
Zoom past the worries, get ready, get quick!
Lollipop castles and marshmallow skies,
This journey's a chuckle, oh, what a surprise!

So mold your own route, where joy can be found,
With a twist and a twirl, let silliness abound!
What matters is you, never fearful to jest,
In the circus of living, just give it your best!

Threads of Desire

With threads made of laughter, stitch your own fate,
A tapestry woven with fruitcake and cake.
Dreams come in flavors, so taste every byte,
From pizza to pudding, just make it feel right.

Pick up that needle, set those wild goals,
Stitch in some chaos, hopscotch on shoals.
Each knot tells a story, each twist is a joke,
A patchwork adventure, with laughter awoke.

Dancing with whims, like a puppet on strings,
Who knew a balloon could grant all of these things?
Let colors collide, throw in sparkles galore,
Your fabric of living is never a bore!

So weave with delight, don't fret or delay,
In the art of existence, be bold, come what may!
With yarns intertwined, seek joy from the start,
This quilt of your wishes is stitched from your heart!

Whispers of the Heart

In a garden of giggles, where wishes take flight,
The whispers of passion can dance in the night.
With butterflies joking, as they flit and they flutter,
Each flutter a chuckle, like bread and fresh butter.

Ponder your options, a buffet of dreams,
With chocolate chip cookies and ice cream in streams.
Giggle at worries, let them float in the air,
Life's too short to frown when you can play fair!

The heart hums a tune, a silly old song,
That makes you want to twirl, and sing all day long.
So listen closely, let your spirit ignite,
In the embrace of this joy, everything feels right.

With each whispered secret, like sprinkles of fun,
Explore the odd corners where mischief has spun.
So leap into laughter, let out a good cheer,
For your heart is the drum, and the dance starts right here

The Compass Within

Twirls and bends, my compass spins round,
Pointing to pizza? Or woodland profound?
A map with no limits, just scribbles and dreams,
Find treasure in giggles, in chocolatey themes.

With a chuckle and wiggle, I'll follow my nose,
To places where silliness sweetly bestows.
A detour to pranks, or a hop on the train,
The more that I wander, the less goes in vain.

Tickle the clouds, or dance with a bee,
The compass inside says, "Just be fully free!"
So fill up with laughter, let whimsy light spark,
For joy is the beacon that shines in the dark.

Wherever it leads, let curiosity guide,
This compass is tricky but ready for a ride.
So grab on tight, friend, let's go have some fun,
For the journey's just started, and it's just begun!

The Unfolding Story

Once there was a cat on a spree,
Chasing dreams of fish in a tree.
It leapt and it tumbled with great flair,
Thinking, 'This is the life I declare!'

A dog joined in with a goofy grin,
Saying, 'Whoa, let's eat before we begin!'
Together they hatched a maddened plot,
To solve the riddle of the perfect spot.

They stumbled upon a mouse in a hat,
Who showed them a map, a marvelous spat.
Off they dashed, a wild trio of fun,
Chasing the sun 'til the day was done.

In this absurd tale, who cares for the goal?
It's the laughs and the chaos that fill up the soul.
As long as there's chocolate and naps in between,
Our story's a riot, the best ever seen!

Mosaic of Aspirations

In a world made of jellybeans and gum,
A penguin danced, having lots of fun.
He dreamt of becoming a rockstar, so grand,
Till he tripped, slid away, and lost his band.

A turtle yelled, 'Hey, don't be so blue!
You're a marshmallow, we believe in you!'
So they formed a band, of misfits and cheer,
Singing songs that were rather unclear.

They toured the land, in their candy-mobile,
With songs about vegtables that made a big deal.
The world laughed along, they'd all sing out loud,
At each silly verse, the crowd just felt proud.

So remember, dear friend, if dreams seem bizarre,
Just dance to the rhythm and be who you are.
Life is a jellybean, peach flavor 'n all,
So bounce in the fun, you'll never fall!

The Fire Within

A fireplace spoke to a curious chair,
'What fuels your jokes? Got any flair?'
The chair just squeaked, 'Well, I do have a lot,
Of people who sit and give all I've got!'

Then a book chimed in, with pages that flipped,
'I'm full of adventures, if only you'd tip!'
The fire just chuckled, 'You think that's the zest?
I spark up the night, I'm simply the best!'

The kettle whistled in a steaming surprise,
'Oh dear, that's just tea for our crazy ties!'
And they all laughed hard, as the night wandered on,
With flavors and tales, their worries were gone.

In a world full of sparks, let your laughter ignite,
Embrace funny moments, they're often the light.
For life's a canvas waiting for play,
Create your own fire, dance silly today!

Colors of Your Spirit

A rainbow once questioned a droopy gray cloud,
'Why are you frowning, you should be so proud!'
The gray just sighed, 'There's no spark in my day,
I need to paint rainbows; oh, what do you say?'

The rainbow replied, with a twist and a twirl,
'Let's splash some colors, in a wild swirl!'
So they gathered hues, both bright and absurd,
Creating a chaos of laughter and words.

They painted the town with they playful spree,
A disco of colors, just wait and see!
With pink polka dots and neon green stripes,
They brought forth a joy that tickled the types.

Now the cloud smiles, laughing cheerfully wide,
Saying, 'I'm fabulous, bursting with pride!'
And in this parade of zany delight,
Find your own colors; your spirit takes flight!

Revelations in Reflection

In a world of cereal and socks,
I ponder my fate amidst the clocks.
Should I chase dreams or just naps?
The struggle is real, like rhymes and chaps.

My dreams are like spaghetti on walls,
They twirl and dance in unpredictable brawls.
Do I want fortune? Or just a snack?
I can't decide—should I go forward or back?

A cat named Whiskers thinks I'm divine,
While I'm out here searching for sunshine.
Maybe I'll code, or make a balloon,
Or just nap with Whiskers under the moon.

Existence can be a real hoot,
With hiccups, belly laughs, and a weird fruit.
So I'll pick my path, whether wise or absurd,
And live like a squirrel chased by a bird.

Map of the Heart

I drew a map in crayon one day,
With squiggles and dots in a fun ballet.
X marks the spot for pizza, you see,
Forget buried treasure; I crave pepperoni!

Adventure awaits in the fridge at night,
Where leftovers glimmer in the pale light.
Should I be brave and eat cold tilapia,
Or sneak a cookie, oh what a mania!

Along the roads of mustard and cheese,
I wander like a child, aiming to please.
Should I take a turn? Or just stick to the bread?
I guess I could nap, right here instead!

The heart leads me where the giggles are loud,
In pizza parlors or juggling crowds.
So I'll follow the laughter, it's where I'll belong,
In this buffet of life, I can't get it wrong!

A Kaleidoscope of Hopes

I took a kaleidoscope to the park,
Where dreams fluttered, even at dark.
A butterfly lands, then flies in a whirl,
Do I chase it? Or trip on a girl?

With wishes stacked high like a cake out of dreams,
I lick my fingers while the sun beams.
Each sprinkles a color, a fluttering cheer,
Should I wear polka dots or stick with my gear?

I've tamed my ambitions like a wild cat,
Sparkling with glitter, or maybe that's fat.
Should I wear a tutu or sport a large hat?
Oh, the choices I make are simply for that!

A rainbow of giggles fills the sky,
I'll juggle my hopes and give it a try.
With laughter as fuel and weird things in tow,
I'll spin through this life—oh, what a show!

Carving My Own Horizon

I'm carving a path with crayons and dreams,
An artist of chaos, or so it seems.
Do I sculpt a turkey or a giant snail?
The only thing certain is my comical fail!

The horizon is bright like a dog in a car,
With flapping ears, it's my guiding star.
Should I follow a trail or paint it neon?
With sprinkles and chaos, I establish my dawn!

A potato with eyes just blinked at me,
As I ponder which path will set me free.
Should I be brave and embrace the unknown?
Or sip lemonade while on my throne?

So here I stand, carving shapes in the sand,
With a side of mischief and a wink, oh so grand.
I'll leap into sunsets with giggles and cheer,
And embrace the absurd, for I persevere!

Flavors of Existence

In a world of jellybeans, I choose the blue,
Cherry on the top, just to make it true.
Pickles on a pizza, oh what a delight,
Life's a buffet, come take a bite!

Carrots wear sunglasses, potatoes in shoes,
Dancing with the broccoli, spreading the news.
Life's a mixed salad, toss it with flair,
Find your own dressing; don't forget the air!

Socks are for wearing, and hats are for laughs,
Kites made of donuts, with sprinkles on halves.
Every day's a canvas, colors galore,
Paint it the way you want, but don't use a door!

So grab a spoon and dive into the fun,
Life's a rollercoaster, just don't forget to run.
Leap over the puddles, trip on the blooms,
Laugh at the journey, and throw out the brooms!

Lanterns in the Mist

When fog rolls in, and lanterns ignite,
Glow-in-the-dark jellybeans take flight.
Chickens in tuxedos, they strut with finesse,
Life's a comedy show, so don't feel distress.

Unicycles carrying monkeys on bikes,
Pigs in pajamas giggling at hikes.
Laughter is cobwebs, catching the light,
Twirl in the shadows, dance through the night.

Balloons with faces, they float overhead,
Invite all the llamas to join in your spread.
A waltz with a cactus, don't step on its toes,
Every twist and turn is where laughter grows.

So bring on the silliness, feast on your dreams,
Paint the town pink with your giggling schemes.
Whatever it is, you can make it your tale,
Life's a buffet, so dig in and sail!

Sculpting Tomorrow

With clay and a grin, I mold my delight,
A unicorn here, and a marshmallow bite.
Pineapples singing, top hats and all,
Sculpting the future, with laughter's call!

A fountain of chocolate, where laughter will flow,
Carve out your wishes, let the giggles grow.
Keep your hands busy, shape dreams with a smile,
Giraffes wearing glasses, they'll stay for a while.

Mountains of giggles, we climb to the sky,
Puddle-jumping puddles, oh my, oh my!
An elephant ballet, spinning around,
In this quirky world, our joy knows no bound.

So take out your chisel, and carve it with grace,
Life's an art project, decorated with lace.
Whatever you dream, just see it unfold,
Sculpt your own laughter, let the stories be told!

Wings of Desire

Butterflies flying in polka-dot suits,
Sipping on rainbows, munching on roots.
A cupcake parade rolls down the lane,
Sweetness and laughter, no room for disdain.

Hop on the back of a glittery frog,
Ride to the stars on a misty fog.
Confetti and jokes, all sprinkled around,
In this giggle-filled world, joy is profound.

Learn to dance with a pillow, do the cha-cha,
Twist with a donut, then sip on a soda.
Sprout silly wings, let your dreams take flight,
In a world painted brightly, everything's right.

So flap your new feathers, soar over the sun,
Giggles are treasures, the best kind of fun.
Whatever you want, just give it a try,
Life's a grand playground, reach for the sky!

Archways to Uncertainty

In the morning, I lose my keys,
Another day with lots of tease.
Should I be a chef or a dancer,
Or maybe just a professional prancer?

I ponder deeply while I eat,
Should I be smart, or just hit repeat?
With cereal as my guiding light,
I chase my dreams with all my might.

Who needs a plan? I'll freestyle it,
A juggler's act—I'll just try it!
With every whim, I'll flip and flop,
In this circus, I just can't stop.

Choices bloom like flowers in spring,
Should I do this or should I sing?
Turning left or going right,
Maybe I'll just nap tonight.

Resonance of the Soul

My heart beats loud—like a bass guitar,
But where's my rhythm? Not a clue so far.
Should I skip stones or paint with flair,
Or simply locate my missing hair?

I call upon my inner sage,
Who's stuck inside a book with no page.
He advises me to follow my nose,
But trust me, it always leads to my toes.

Spaghetti or painting, which way to go?
One gets saucy, the other a show!
I'll ride the waves of choice galore,
But what if I tumble? I might just snore.

I'll throw a dart at my big ol' map,
And laugh as I plan my next big nap.
In this dance, forgive the twirl,
For uncertainty's my favorite whirl.

The Awakening of Dreams

In my slumber, I see wild things,
Like cats in capes and birds with rings.
Should I chase dreams or let them flee,
Maybe just order pizza, you see?

Dancing with marshmallows, oh what a sight,
Should I be a hero or a knight?
Cooking pasta or learning to glide,
With all these choices—it's hard to decide!

I scribble my thoughts in rainbow pens,
Vowing to be the life of my friends.
Pancakes stacked like a tower so tall,
Will I conquer breakfast? I'll give it my all!

Letting my whims take the lead,
I pull a card: "What do you need?"
To dream of this, or to dream of that,
I'll take a nap, then see where I'm at.

A Spectrum of Intent

Bubbles float and dreams collide,
Should I slide down a rainbow slide?
With colors bursting, I take a sip,
Of fizzy ideas that twist and flip.

Should I dive into a pool of goo,
Or run in circles, trying something new?
Each choice is like a silly dance,
As I try to make the most of chance.

I chase the sun, but fall in shade,
Is this where I should be—unmade?
With ice cream dreams and candy canes,
I ride this wave through sunny plains.

I wave goodbye to the serious frown,
And wear a hat made of upside-down.
Whatever happens, I'll greet with glee,
Uncertain? Sure! But fancy and free.